5/03

Bessie Coleman

Daring to Fly

by Sally M. Walker

illustrations by Janice Lee Porter

Carolrhoda Books, Inc./Minneapolis

The photograph on p. 46 appears courtesy of the Smithsonian National Air and Space
Museum (neg. #80–12873). The quotation on p. 41 is taken from: Rich, Doris L. *Queen
Bess*. Washington, D.C.: Smithsonian Institution Press, 1993.

This book is available in two editions:
Library binding by Carolrhoda Books, Inc., a division of Lerner Publishing Group
Soft cover by First Avenue Editions, an imprint of Lerner Publishing Group
241 First Avenue North
Minneapolis, MN 55401 U.S.A.

Website address: www.lernerbooks.com

Library of Congress Cataloging-in-Publication Data

Walker, Sally M.
    Bessie Coleman : daring to fly / by Sally M. Walker ; illustrations by Janice Lee
Porter.
      p.   cm. — (On my own biography)
    Summary: Describes the life and accomplishments of Bessie Coleman, who
overcame racism and poverty to become the first African American woman pilot.
    ISBN: 0–87614–919–0 (lib. bdg. : alk. paper)
    ISBN: 0–87614–103–3 (pbk. : alk. paper)
    1. Coleman, Bessie, 1896–1926—Juvenile literature. 2. Air pilots—United States—
Biography—Juvenile literature. 3. African American women air pilots—Biography—
Juvenile literature. [1. Coleman,Bessie, 1896–1926. 2. Air pilots. 3. African
Americans—Biography. 4. Women—Biography.] I. Porter, Janice Lee, ill. II. Title.
III. Series.
TL540646 W35   2003
629.13'092—dc21   2002004676

Manufactured in the United States of America
1 2 3 4 5 6 – JR – 08 07 06 05 04 03

Ready to Fly
Waxahachie, Texas, 1902

Bessie Coleman's fingers bled.

Her back hurt.

Picking cotton was tough work
for a 10-year-old.

Bessie stared at the next picker's sack.

It dragged on the ground
as he pulled it along.

It looked like a good place to rest.

Stealing a ride on a cotton sack
was just the kind of daring thing
that Bessie Coleman would do.

PLOP! Down she went.

Bessie hated picking cotton,
but she didn't have much choice.
The Colemans were poor.
Mama needed all the money
that Bessie could earn.
The only good part of the day was the end.
Then Bessie got to do math,
which she loved.

She added up how much cotton
her family had picked.
The Colemans got paid by the pound.
If the white man who paid them
tried to cheat, Bessie wasn't afraid
to set him straight.
She was *that* daring.

When the cotton season ended,
Bessie was glad to get back to school.
She went to a one-room school
for African American children.
In 1902, white children and black children
couldn't go to the same schools.
Most schools for black children
had little money.
Bessie's school had few books.
Sometimes the teacher ran out
of paper and pencils.
Still, Bessie worked hard.
She planned to do more with
her life than pick cotton.
The more she learned,
the better her chances would be.

Bessie didn't work all the time.

When the library wagon came around,

Mama rented books for her to read.

At night, Bessie read out loud.

She loved the story of Harriet Tubman.

Now there was a daring black woman!

She had led hundreds of slaves to freedom.
Harriet Tubman had certainly done
important things with her life.
As she read, Bessie made up her mind.
Someday *she* would do
something important, too.

In 1910, Bessie was 18 years old.

She started college in Oklahoma,

but her money ran out.

She went home to Texas

and washed clothes to earn more.

While Bessie scrubbed and ironed,

she thought about the future.

If she wanted to amount to something,

she would have to leave Waxahachie.

She decided to go live

with her brothers in Chicago.

Surely such a big city would offer

a chance for a new life.

Dreaming of Flight
Chicago, 1919

Bessie was hopping mad.
Her brother John was teasing her
at the barbershop where she worked.
John had fought in France
during World War I.
The women there were better than
Chicago's black women, he joked.
Some French women even flew airplanes.
Who could imagine a black woman
flying an airplane?
Bessie knew that she could do
whatever she set her mind to.

Soaring high above the ground
sounded daring and important—
just right for Bessie Coleman.
She decided then and there
that she would prove John wrong.

In 1919, flying an airplane
was a new kind of dream.
People had been flying only since 1903.
Airplanes weren't used much for travel.
In many places, they were so rare
that people ran outside to watch
if one flew overhead.
Hardly any airplane pilots were women.
And none of the women pilots were black.

Bessie wished she could ask a black pilot
to teach her to fly.
But no black pilots lived near Chicago.
She went from airfield to airfield,
asking white pilots to teach her.
Every single one said no.
Some refused because she was black.
Others refused because she was a woman.

Bessie didn't give up.

She asked Robert Abbott for help.

He was one of her customers

at the barbershop.

Robert was smart and wealthy.

He ran his own newspaper,

the *Chicago Defender*.

Go to France, Robert told Bessie.
In France, white people treated
black people as equals.
She could find a teacher there.
A ticket to France would be expensive.
So would flying lessons.
Bessie got busy.
She found a better-paying job
running a chili shop.
She took French lessons.
She dreamed about flying.
And in November 1920, Bessie boarded
a ship and steamed off to France.

Takeoff!
Le Crotoy, France, 1920

Bessie ran her hand lightly
over the side of the airplane.
She could hardly believe it.
She was 28 years old,
and her first day of flying lessons
had come at last.
Bessie checked the propeller and the tires.
She looked for tears and cracks
in the cloth-covered wings.
Good pilots always checked their planes
before takeoff.

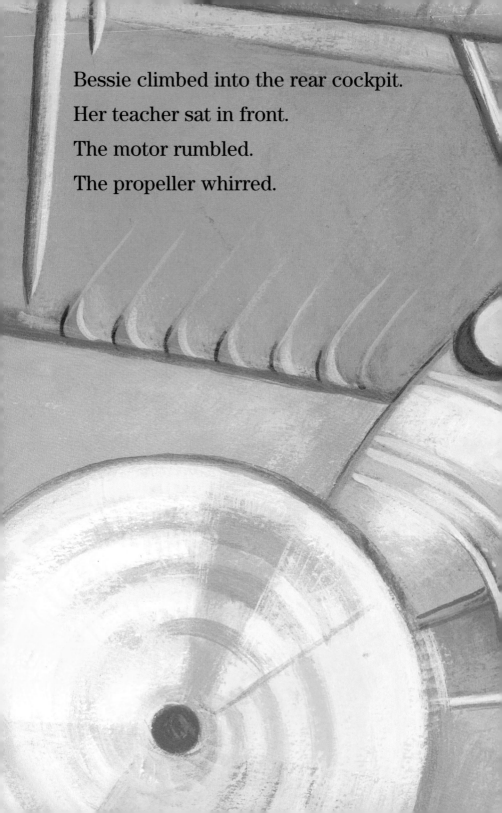

Bessie climbed into the rear cockpit.

Her teacher sat in front.

The motor rumbled.

The propeller whirred.

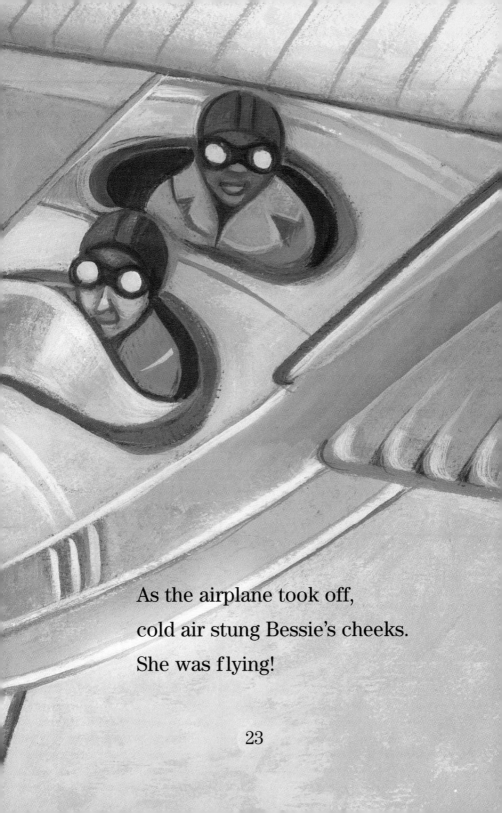

As the airplane took off,
cold air stung Bessie's cheeks.
She was flying!

After that first lesson,

Bessie practiced hard and kept learning.

Then one day, she saw a classmate

die in a crash.

Bessie was shocked.

Her dream was putting her in danger.

Still, she wasn't about to give up.

She worked even harder

on her flying skills.

With each trip to the sky,

Bessie grew more daring.

Soon she was flying on her own.

Seven months of hard work paid off.
In June 1921, Bessie earned
a pilot's license.
Now she could fly anywhere in the world.
She was the first African American
woman to get a pilot's license.

Her brother John had been wrong after all.
And Bessie had made something
of herself at last.
It was time to go home
and show the world what
Bessie Coleman could do.

Watch Me Fly!

Long Island, New York, September 1922

Bessie gave her boots one last polish.

A band started to play.

The jazzy music matched her mood.

For the first time,

she was going to fly in front of

an American crowd.

More than a thousand people had paid

to see her take to the sky.

29

Bessie climbed into the cockpit
and pulled her goggles over her eyes.
A co-pilot climbed in back.
The mechanic started the engine.
The crowd stared as the plane rolled
across the field and left the ground.
In the 1920s, airplanes often crashed.

Everyone knew that even flyers
with experience sometimes crashed.
Would this black woman pilot be safe?
Bessie soared high above the crowd.
She glided through the air and landed easily.
A perfect flight!

Soon Bessie was doing more
than just flying.
She thrilled her fans with amazing stunts.
In Chicago, she glided so low over
the crowd that people ducked.
They gazed at the plane as it curved upward.

Suddenly, it turned sharply to the side.

The audience gasped.

Had Bessie lost control?

Not for a second!

She turned the plane again

and completed a smooth figure 8.

Bessie's dives and rolls scared some people.
She was risking her life with those
daring stunts, they said.
But Bessie saw herself as a flying actress.
Her job was to show people a good time.
She had another reason to take chances.
She needed to earn money.

Bessie wanted to open a flying school.
She would need planes
and a place to keep them.
Those things would be expensive.
Flying for crowds was the best way
to pay for them.

Bessie hoped that her school would help
other black people make their
dreams of flight come true.
She worked hard to earn
the money to open it.
To win more fans,
Bessie gave talks at churches
and theaters.

She talked to newspaper reporters, too.
Sometimes she stretched the truth
about her career as a pilot.
She told one reporter that she had flown
in six countries in Europe!
But there was nothing fake
about Bessie's flying.
It was magnificent.

In 1923, Bessie went to California,

full of plans for her flight school.

She bought her first airplane.

It was a small, used plane

called a Curtiss Jenny.

Then she set up an air show.

As she always did, Bessie checked

her plane before taking off.

Everything looked fine.

She flew the Jenny 300 feet into the air.

Suddenly, the motor stalled.

The plane nose-dived toward the ground.

This dive was no stunt.

The Jenny crashed with Bessie inside.

Rescuers rushed Bessie to the hospital.

She had broken a leg and several ribs.

Cuts covered her face and hands.

But she was alive.

Bessie spent almost three months in bed.

She was bruised and in pain.

Her leg itched inside the cast.

Worst of all, her plane had been

completely destroyed.

But Bessie wouldn't give up.

She sent her fans a message from the hospital.

"As soon as I can walk I'm going to fly!"

Bessie kept her word.
That September, she went
to Columbus, Ohio.
She borrowed a plane
and set up another show.

If Bessie was nervous about flying again,

she didn't show it.

Ten thousand fans were thrilled

to see her soar into the sky.

This time, not a thing went wrong.

Bessie looked forward to the future.
She was ready to fly in more shows.
Maybe she would try parachuting
or a few other fancy tricks.

One way or another, she would keep working
to open her flight school.
And she would help keep the dream of flight
alive for women and men of all races.

Afterword

Bessie Coleman went on to perform air shows in many places, including her hometown of Waxahachie, Texas. Along with her death-defying stunts as a pilot, she learned to parachute. She also wing-walked, balancing herself on the wings of a moving plane while another pilot took the controls. Everywhere she went, she amazed and inspired thousands of fans.

Sadly, Bessie did not live to see all her dreams come true. In 1926, a terrible accident ended her life. Bessie was preparing to do a parachute jump from a Jenny in Florida. A wrench fell into the plane's control gears and jammed them. The pilot lost control. From her seat in the rear cockpit, Bessie could do nothing to help. The plane crashed. Both Bessie and the pilot died.

Although she died before she could open her flight school, the daring young cotton picker from Texas did indeed do something important with her life. In spite of unfair treatment, she became the first African American woman to earn a pilot's license. Her skill inspired many fans to become pilots themselves. And her determination and courage inspired people of all races to aim high to achieve their goals.

Important Dates

1892—Bessie Coleman was born in a one-room cabin in Atlanta, Texas, on January 26. (The exact year of her birth is not known for certain.)

1894—Family moved to Waxahachie, Texas

1910—Studied at the Colored Agricultural and Normal University in Langston, Oklahoma; ran out of money; returned to Waxahachie

1915—Moved to Chicago

1917—Married Claude Glenn

1920—Traveled to France to attend flight school

1921—Earned pilot's license, becoming the first African American woman to do so

1922—Continued flying lessons in France; gave first air show in Long Island, New York

1923—Crashed in California; spent almost three months in hospital

1926—Died in plane crash in Jacksonville, Florida

1995—The United States Postal Service issued a stamp honoring Bessie Coleman's role in the history of flight.